*Courtney,
with love and gratitude,
Shannon. ♡
11·22·23*

green card girl

poetry

~~shannon wolf~~

Copyright © 2023 Shannon Wolf

All rights reserved. No part of this publication may be reproduced, distributed, or transmitted in any form or by any means, including photocopying, recording, or other electronic or mechanical methods, without the prior written permission of the publisher, except in the case of brief quotations embodied in critical reviews and certain other noncommercial uses permitted by copyright law. For permission requests, write to the publisher at the address below.

ELJ Editions, Ltd. is committed to publishing works of quality and integrity. In that spirit, we are proud to offer this poetry collection to our readers. Names, characters, places, and incidents either are the product of the author's imagination or are used fictitiously, and any resemblance to actual persons, living or dead, business establishments, events, or locales is entirely coincidental.

ISBN: 978-1-942004-65-3

Library of Congress Control Number: 2023947529

Cover Design by Shannon Wolf

ELJ Editions, Ltd.
P.O. Box 815
Washingtonville, NY 10992

www.elj-editions.com

Praise for *Green Card Girl*

"There are odes in this marvelous collection – to chicken wings, to Tony Soprano, to the poet's husband's Toyota – but really, every poem here is an ode. Shannon Wolf writes hymns of praise to all things, for they've all helped form a voice that is sensitive, observant, and, more than anything, grateful. *Green Card Girl* salutes past and present lives, yes, but it also tips its beret to the lives that are to come."

- David Kirby, author of *The House on Boulevard St.*

"Shannon Wolf's debut collection is incandescent, a transnational anthem about family trauma and the universal desire for selfhood. Through requiem and elegy and humor, Wolf's poems navigate the complicated geographies of the inherited self and explore, with grace and devastating wit, the challenging process of unbecoming, of being found, of finding love when all seems lost. Beyond the 'land of no mothers' and the hollowing fatherlessness that haunts these poems, *Green Card Girl* also reminds us that there is forgiveness in becoming. Arguing that the body—however ravaged, however abused—is a fundamentally sacred place, Wolf crafts a powerful warning in these pages: *Do not allow others to poison your precious real estate; forge your own peace. You deserve it.* Guaranteed to make you laugh and cry, Wolf is refreshing and raw and obliterates expectations of what a poem is and can do."

-Tara Stillions Whitehead, author of *The Year of the Monster*

"A classic American story of dreams and immigration. But more than that, *Green Card Girl* is a chronicle of pain, disappointment, and the baggage 'so moveable & immovable,' that we carry. Ultimately, Wolf's story is about survival and love, and anyone who has ever yearned for home will find a fellow traveler in Wolf."

- Eric Nguyen, author of *Things We Lost to the Water*

"Shannon Wolf invites the reader into a past so fiercely nostalgic for its future. Daring, ferocious, and tender, *Green Card Girl* grapples with hope and disappointment, leaving behind Glasgow pubs and Domino's delivery drivers to forge a distinct new world of belonging. Don't sleep on this stunning debut."

- Gauraa Shekhar, author of *Notes*

"Shannon Wolf's *Green Card Girl* is a searching, searing collection of dreams and desires. At every turn, these poems are "trying to find a way to get home," to a place of belonging. Through clever craft and sheer force of will, the poems in *Green Card Girl* deliver a multi-part harmony of placemaking, love, and longing for what might be out there, "waiting for me." This is a debut that moves with fierce courage and sonorous language."

- Dan Brady, author of *Songs in E—*

for Thornton Albert Wolf

Contents

arrival

—

Just Happy to Be Here	3
Welcome to Your American Dream	4
Gallery of Chronic Illness	6
It Doesn't Rain Here Like They Said	7
My First Date in Two Years	9
National Anthem	10
Neighborhood Aubade	11
Silphium	12
An Engagement	13

—

"I'm on the lookout for hope"	17
Neverland	18
White Picket Fence	19
Marriage	20
And Then I Was American With Him	21
On The Gulf	24
Good Wives	25
Green Card Girl	26

—

before
—

Mother Tongue	31
Wings	33
Be Our Guest	34
Tennyson Insurance	35
When You Sit in the Pews of a Church, What Do You Pray For?	36
Code Brown	37
Elizabeth, Everywhere	39
Where We Started	40
The Hold-Steady	42
Little Town Blues	43
Ode to Tony Soprano	44
Calling All Cars	45
Storage	46
To Greg, My Domino's Delivery Driver	47
Before My Esophagus Tore and I Retched Black Blood	48
Leap of Faith	49

onward
—

Reading in the Tub	55
Tabula Rasa	56

Ode to My Husband's Toyota	57
After You Gave Birth	58
New Year's Resolution	59
I Don't Know What You Want Me To Say	60
Kisatchie	61
Tale As Old As Time	62
Eleven Delights from Lockdown	63
Memory of a Dragon	64
Taking Communion	66
After the Hurricane with Carly Rae Jepsen	67
The Vulnerability of Estrangement	68
Unconditional	69

When I Cut Ties With My Father, My Family Forgets Me Like I'm Fiction	73
What is This Place, If Not a Nest?	74
Are All The Fathers In Your Poems Real?	76
Nothing But Memory is Left	77
When people ask: *How would it feel to move back to England?*	78
I Can Forgive You	79
We are all writing about the moon actually	80
On My 29th Birthday	81

Ode to My Husband's Ass	82
To All The Towns I Loved Before	83
Homecoming	84
Roots	85

arrival

9th July 2018

By the time you turn twenty-six, you will have lived in twenty-nine different houses in England. You had the small rooms where the bedroom doors couldn't shut, with the leftover furniture and the overloaded bookcases. You had the cabin bed in the 'boy' colors, with postcards from the cinema taped high on the wall, a torch wedged at the side of the mattress. Everything smelled like smoke but none of you knew until you left. Last year you cried almost every day, usually behind the wheel of your car on your way to some insurance job. You haven't spoken to your mother for almost five years. Your car wheezed its last breath and gave up on the side of the road between Lancaster and London. You drove a rented van back to Ilminster with everything you owned inside and packed it all away into your father's garage. It felt like the whole country was telling you to leave.

Your thirtieth house is in America. In Seattle. You will sleep in a basement bedroom. Everything will be different there. Like fresh air. You leave today. You can forget home if you want. Nothing there changes anyway.

Fun fact: Seattle is 4741 miles from Ilminster. Of course, Ilminster isn't really the problem. Do you ever wish you could pick up a town and shake half the people out of it? Why am I asking you? Of course, you do.

Just Happy to Be Here

Down by the water, in FremontI can breathe I can breathe
surveying the dipping boats
dressed in white like brides
the blue bridge peeking at the sky
I will be weightless in Lake Union
my swimsuit will be heavier than my skin
my fingers splayed in wonder
the seaweed of my hair
drifting in the current
No memory no landno England weighing on my chest
<u>& I am learning my language again</u>
<u>It's all the same except when it's not</u>
<u>crisps are chips</u>
<u>& apologies are fewer</u>I smile more easily
the ride home would be long
but I won't be taking it
Told everyone I'm here for good
the colors are new

Yes blue is brighter here whereI can see I can see

Welcome to Your American Dream

On the plane, you sat beside Kimmy & Carlos:
strangers who shared a Dunkin' cup filled
with vodka & screwed in the tight cove
of the plane bathroom. Kimmy whispered
that the sex was fast & unsatisfying & Carlos
pointed out the Mississippi River to you
as you passed above it like a gull. You felt
young beside them. When you landed in Seattle
you all walked to the luggage carousel,
arms linked as if you were all high on Pacific air
as you met your new boss, smiling & blonde,
clutching a sign with your name in glitter glue.

You had never seen a blue sky like that first day
at Matthews Beach. You're a nanny for now,
& the children turn their faces to aquamarine
with icing from a sheet cake. The oldest
has been doing a fake British accent since
you arrived. You attended a neighbor's cookout,
your feet in a paddling pool filled with sliced
lemons & plucked daisy heads, white as milk.
You toasted s'mores in your new backyard
& stepped out late at night to see the blood moon.
Life feels too easy. No one has told you
to lower your voice since you left England.

A few weeks in, you went to a tattoo parlor
on Roosevelt. Under the watchful eye of a bear
holding nunchucks, a bald man tattooed
the Seattle skyline on the soft part of your arm.
You'll come to regret it when people assume
the ink is a reference to Frasier or Grey's Anatomy.
In two years you tell a friend with the same tattoo
how much that bothers you, & they reply *mine
is a Frasier tattoo* & you sink through the floor.
When you got home with your new scar, your boss
was shocked by your impulse, impressed

by your spontaneity. You were unknowable.

You spent time writing in Suzzallo Library,
eyes up at the vast eaves, feeling small &
important in your Beach Boys tee, your golden
laptop fragile on the desk. You flip-flopped
into the university district & drank cool glasses
of coke. Your body alone in bar windows
solitary & warm in the slow Washington sun.
On weekdays you were patient & prepared,
in black leggings & sensible shoes. On weekends
you waited for America to disappoint you
but it never did. You forgot to call your father
or text friends. Maybe they all stopped existing.

America is everything you knew it would be.
You never planned on Seattle. You always
thought it would be New York, which is
the first tattoo you got, without telling anyone,
one dark morning in Chichester when you were
still miserable in a cruel, grueling relationship.
After a month or so you have a truck & driving
on the right side feels as if you had always done it.
You bought a baseball hat. People back home
start saying you sound like a Yank. You recall
your father at Gatwick airport: *You must come home
in a year.* You said: *I'm never coming back.*

Gallery of Chronic Illness
Or Finding a Doctor in America is Really Hard

I want us to wake up in the future
and take pills like aliens
clockwork every day
and never need to sleep;
we'd regenerate all the time.
I sleep late every chance I get
and I hate the sleep and how it takes
its measure of my head. Pain behind
my eyes from morning beam
neon-bright, glow of noon, sting of night.

I could move the notebooks,
the pizza boxes, the laundry
from the empty side
to hide the evidence
that this bed sleeps one despite
being big enough for two.
If I could take a pill,
never sleep again,
I'd make up the bedsheets
neat on both sides
and encase this room in glass:
an installation of what I left behind.

It Doesn't Rain Here Like They Said

If it did, I wouldn't buy an umbrella. It's just not done.
Not across the seven hills of Seattle, unless you're a tourist.

In Pioneer Square I stopped walking to eat lunch standing up.
A woman and a man screamed at each other, tents packed away,

slung over their shoulders. I do not intervene, observant and green,
but when he walks away, I offer the woman my spare warm soda.

Her hair is uncombed but less unkempt than my own. Her blue eyes
are wild. We walked down First Avenue in companionable quiet.

—

I drove along Mercer Street in a car with four children, none mine.
The red light I ran flowered on my cheeks. The oldest girl cringed

up front. The man in uniform chuckled, made casual conversation.
Doesn't he know I think he is a killer? My hands locked on the wheel, gun

at his vicious hip as I had imagined him. I heard a tooth
was discovered on this street, belonging to a mammoth, older

than I can fathom. As I drove off I swore never to take that street again,
but, it's hardest to keep promises that you make to yourself.

—

I went to Alki Beach as soon as I had the car to myself but I couldn't
get close enough to the lighthouse to see it. My hair became heavy

with crystals of salt. A woman sat beside me on a bench and asked
for my number. I flushed pink and gave it but I suppose she had heard

my accent and thought I'd work under the table. I blocked her number
before I left and felt embarrassed for months about it. What's the point

of a lighthouse you can't see? I heard it was once just one man
and a kerosene lamp but I suppose you could say that about anything.

—

My life is ordinary. I drop off and pick up children from a school
where they speak Spanish all day and sometimes I leave the car parked

and walk part-way around Green Lake, algae blooms like fireworks
deep down. In a twenty-minute turn, I counted seventy-eight dogs.

I eat private muffins from my tote bag and break my own shoes.
Old white men practice qigong on the grass and I stand on the steps

of the bathhouse and imagine walking into the water fully clothed.
If I sound sad, I'm not. I just didn't expect this. I was promised rain.

My First Date in Two Years
with thanks to the Fiddler's Inn, Seattle

              Sitting at a table for two my mind rolling double-time
       this isn't meant to happen yet   Your breath sounds like windchimes
           America America America   I've only been here two months
but here you are with eyes of Aegean mud   you know I get stuck every time
   I only see you in encyclopedic places   the library the bookstore behind my eyes
      I'm not supposed to find you so fast   What's the catch
The shape of your mouth   it's the sand through my fingers it's the tang of orange
           stinging my lip when I was half this size
  No I don't want to hook up back at your place   that's really not what I'm saying
       I'm saying that I believe I will be waking up to windchimes
  when I am eighty-something years old   & I never knew until you lifted your glass
             & I saw your evening wrists turned to the light

National Anthem
for George Wolf Sr.

Though I never knew him,
there's something in your father's eyes
in that shot,
behind his glasses,
a hint of wry that I see in you,
your sarcasm, your graveled wit,
I see it in your blue world eyes,
where I paint myself onto your map.

There is a way that you breathe
when no one is watching,
like every breath is considered
and counted and coveted,
and I covet you,
my American dream
in flannel shirts and blue jeans.

I take a sip of you and quench
and cannot quench.
I feel where you are
when the rooms are dark
and there is only your chest rising,
your hand, clothed in sleep,
outstretched for the company of England.

Neighborhood Aubade

Who lived in houses like these
Unglazed sun burnishing ligneous front doors
hoop facing out into the street // year-round Christmas lights
lego brick chimneys line the cusp of dawn
chipped paint and fallen down fences // snoopy inflatables and frog ceramics

In the half-light through swollen eyes you whispered: *I want to say it*

Oh, we loved in houses like these
You on bended knee in the bedroom baked in the half-light
then opening the french doors // out on the deck quiet in our rocking
your dusky eyelashes against my sunshine mouth
the most fragile part of you // home on the bodies of my lips

Silphium

They found the seventy-six statues
left at Cyrene, and were there coins
scattered at their feet, bearing the signs
of the herb? Did the shapes reveal that
something like love might be there still?

I would whisper to the hedgerows
of the days when I would leave home
and though I knew nothing of that ancient land
or the smell of silphium, I knew
I was coming here, to this city,
where they sell Christmas trees from concrete lots,
where the burnt-neon buses run through the night,
where there are smaller cities inside the big city,
made of tents and trolleys and trash.

I knew I was headed your way,
that to make that perfect ideograph
our valves would be made ready
to be ripped from us and combined.
Carthage and Alexandria drove Cyrene to ruin
and Cyrene harvested silphium until there was no more
but with a doodle of your initials, I capture the shape
and there is love still, here, on the other side of the world.

An Engagement
after Arthur Aron's test, 1997

We are a floating bed
                        in a pooling of light
                                              buoyed up by the windows' whites
                legs on legs, chests and thinking heads
                                                      We said all the answers
                the questions torn from a page
                          We kissed through the paragraphs a word at a time
And to think we could not hold a gaze for four minutes
                      without making this a bed of quicksand
                              and sinking
                                  down
                                    in
                                      it
  So answer me this as you lay on my chest   {widows in paradise playing so soft}
     why must we go out to work
                when this love;
                        it's so easy

11th November 2018

Can you believe this is your life? Can you believe it? You want to write to a younger you and tell her all the gold is coming if she will just open her hands. So you do write, from his bed with the curtains streaming and the snow coming in with the wind. Don't look away. This is what you have asked for, cried for, and begged for. Didn't you pray once for this? Don't you deserve this? When you wake up beside him, tell yourself thank you for getting there. Thank you.

Actually, the first moment of peace you had was before you met him, standing on the bank of Lake Union, under the shadow of the Fremont Bridge, taking in a sky so blue you don't believe it's the same one they had at home. Afternoons you spend driving, ferrying children to appointments and games, and at night you stand under the neon pall of the drive-in and eat burgers in your white truck. You could swear that blue sky fell down and hung right there, in his eyes, just for you.

Emily Brontë wrote: "Whatever our souls are made of, his and mine are the same," and that's a classic quote of course, but you think more often of what Elton John wrote: "Laughing like children, living like lovers, rolling like thunder under the covers."

"I'm on the lookout for hope"

says some man on the internet, no one to me at all.
For some reason, I feel like crying, and I do.

Because what was I looking for? When I watched
the snow visible only in the lamplight outside my house

or when I took photographs in the dark to prove
I still existed? I was on the lookout for hope back there

and now I walk the streets of Seattle and want to grab
every stranger by the shoulders and shake them and ask:

Do you see it? I can feel it here, enveloping me, bright.
My throat is no longer mottled and grey, it is golden.

My body is long and beautiful, an unfurling map
that shows all the places I've been, all the bites

and bruises still part of my skin. Part of me still stands
in Kendal, in Chichester, in Ilminster, waiting. Permission

isn't coming, I know. Do you know people speak with loud voices
here and no one is ashamed? When I drive alone in the afternoon

I feel as if I have wings like they were there all along, forcing
their way up my spine and breaking out like applause.

Neverland

We are the lost boys darling   Our mothers
are out there somewhere   We're missing
here together   in a land of no mothers
There are no women in oversized necklaces here
no emptied bottles of chardonnay on our island
Can I give you a thimble Can I give you a kiss
Wasn't everything hard & unfamiliar before this

You have all these brothers   & sisters
Did they ever binocular   the second star to the right
Did they ever go straight on until morning
Because here it has been just you & me honey
Can we keep it this way   I see mermaids
in your eyes   you see pirates in mine
        Are we the lost ones darling
Think happy thoughts   I can't fly worth a damn
I give you this ring   so give me your hand

White Picket Fence
wedgwood, seattle

me a woman	in sweats surveying the neighborhood from my driveway
a man jogging	
a man striding	his wife ten paces behind groceries paper-bagged
	in her arms like a child
a man leaf blowing	cheeks ruddy with afternoon liquor
a man dousing a lawn	with a hose looped loosely around his spraying arm
a man in a chevy	
a man slowbrakes	beside the trailer in the spaces outside my house
	looks up at it looks over at me and back again
	his mouth a snaking line
a man in a honda	
a man in a pontiac	
a man who pauses	sees me alone
	his body gunning toward me
	his mouth a knife
	but turning to a grimaced smile over my head
	a nod a going on his way
a man my husband	opening the garden gate hammer and gloves in hand

Marriage

When your hand
tightens at the curve
of my warm side
in your sleep,
the handkerchief
edges of your fingers
lacing over my protrusion
of stomach,
I think in half-sleep
how sweet it is
to not need
to breathe it in,
to not take a pound back.
In your sleep
you always reply
when I say the words.
Sometimes we text
I love you two—
because there's two of us.
In daylight
your everyday hands
rub circles
on my back
in the checkout line
or while watching tv
your evening hands
squeezing mine
so tight I think
my laughter
might burst
from our palms.
You kiss my shoulder
in your sleep:
I am loved
just like this.

And Then I Was American With Him

Before my first date with my husband,
I stood him up twice; why he still came
that Friday, honestly I'll never know.
I cry once a day about the distant idea
that he might someday die. Believe me,
I would tear out a lung, a liver, even
all of my straight black eyelashes
to have those wasted two days back.

I'd flood the British Isles to repeat
the two days that followed with him
in a Portland motel where the cashier
mistook me for a prostitute and asked
if we wanted the room by the hour;
its walls were the color of warm shit.
Next door, the Tik Tok Lounge
played a movie projection, yellow

and flickering as we drank fudgsicles
at 2 am and I fell in love with him.
He could read my mind, my words
in his voice through the night, his
fingertips on the apples of my cheeks.
The first time he made love to me
the sweat from his glowing face
fell on my body in the sultry dark
like a rainfall in some far-off arid land.

—

Thornton unwraps his new robe
in some hotel room in Nashville.
Later today after he drinks gin,
whiskey and brandy, we'll write
our names inside a hardback book
and leave it in the bar, and then
I will be the one to fall down

in the street. He will help me

back into this bed and fall asleep,
one quiet hand on my stomach
as I bandage my concrete-grey knee.
Now though, he preens in plaid,
playing model for my camera.
It is his birthday. I tell him *undress*,
and to slide the robe on when
his body is bare. He slinks back in

to find me naked, no makeup,
up on my still-smooth knees.
He undoes the belt, twirling it
like a baton, and I hum some
bad burlesque tune for him
to strip to. His hips shake
and I scream *honey take it off!*
When he pins me on the bed
the whole hotel hears us laughing.

——

The last time I had diarrhea
and shit myself perching
on our living room couch,
Thornton came to roost on
the ledge of the tub, watching
as I washed my soiled knickers
by hand, kneading the fabric
into china-white soap blossoms

the same way that he kneads
pizza dough on Friday nights.
We stumble to our bedroom
hand in hand like school kids
to lay on the bed chortling
about moon kittens, teddy
bears and costumed men
climbing out of oil paintings.

Clad in pajamas covered with elk
he tells me he is riled as if
he has been radicalized until
our giggles erupt in unison.
A sacred language we molded
together: photographs in cork
albums, leftover arugula flowering
right outside our front door
and pink post-its on every wall.

—

After seven months together
Thornton put a ring on my finger
on a courthouse roof in Seattle.
Once the judge said *kiss the bride*
we both whispered *holy shit*,
and then I was American with him.
He says *oi* and *car bonnet* for me,
I refuse to say *a-loo-minum* aloud

but I do swap *plasters* for *band aids*.
Our life is a purple-pink sky
and in a month or two we'll pack
everything we own into boxes
and we'll move to another city.
There will be sprinklers on sidewalks,
pastrami sandwiches at noon and
Thornton's smile on our front porch.

These gentle days I am forgetting
England: all its grey bodies, tiny skies
and muzzled silence. I flood the truck
with radio, windows down as I waltz us
up the highway; an unexpected ballerina,
Thornton's hand squeezing my knee.
Now I know why I had to come here.
It was never this land, calling over the sea
—I knew he was waiting for me.

On the Gulf

Chocolate chip pancakes as thick as my fist,
pink tulips misheard as orange carnations,
rasping pages of old books piled in the window,
you refilling my water glass until beads gather.

>The house would be empty without you in it.
>No, really it would be empty, completely.
>I'd sit on the balcony, smoke cigarettes all night,
>daub the embers in a ceramic ramekin,
>write poems that I'd crumple and burn,
>sleep with the television for muffled company.

No. I prefer smoking on the balcony *with* you,
after swimming in the pool. Long lazy evenings,
you carry me on your back in the warm water,
my arms wrapped around your shoulders.
This apartment is a cocoon and we are spinning
our web together, glistening like twinkle lights.

>Twenty seven years, full lungs, stacked baggage
>All that, you carry   and I am weightless.

Good Wives

Call me soft if you want, call me nostalgic.
It's Christmas so I'm reading *Little Women* again.
Jo is in her garret on her red bolster pillow,
in a deerstalker cap and at once, I am ten,
back against the four-burner Aga oven,
my ballerina feet flat on the threadbare carpet.
Here was Jo before her locks were shorn off,
before she took her lumps,
before a Bhaer was made out of her.
Here was Shannon before she grew six inches,
before she rolled with the punches,
before a Wolf was made out of her.
Jo slept with progress under her pillow,
Shannon had her castles in the air, even then.
I remember how Jo hid with Laurie
watching dancers from an alcove,
watching her sister's pretty ankles turn,
the smooth way he took her wrist
to turn her about the room,
And now I picture us, my husband and I,
dancing to *moon river* in the dining room,
my clumsy feet and his hand on the small
of my back. How he had said yes
to dance classes when I expected him
to laugh and say no. How when we dance now
it is some riff on the Cajun two-step,
far from Jo's frigid Concord winters.
No, it is not snowing here in Louisiana
but in these pages, there is frost
and lost gloves and wet feet.
And there is dancing, here and there.

Green Card Girl

I

To come to you—I navigated bitter winds
    crossed oceans blind
        told the old world: I rescind.

To be with you—I renounced my name
    faced down suited men
        left the birthing hips, never to return again.

To sink into you—I sat in the waiting room
    on hallowed ground
        swore the oath and hoped to bloom.

To be part of you—I perched with ankles tight
    my life in a file
        breath caught, sweating under the spotlight.

To be alone with you —I swear down
    I'd swim across this land
        I'd give my body to this ancient ground

    I pledge allegiance. No turning back now.

II

Before I got here and before you got here, there was a whole world here, canvassing the land from mountain ledge to chiseled valley. And now, I stand here and ask to stay and ask to stay and ask to stay. Some do not get to ask the question, do not get to hear an answer, do not get to untie the bouquet from its brown paper, cut the stems, and sink them in water. Some are left in the waiting room, in the waiting room, in the waiting room and there I am, on a university campus clutching a forty dollar textbook that I will only read ten pages of, toting keys to a car that became mine simply because I fell in love. There I am, not waiting but being introduced by my professor at readings as *our very own green card girl*. Before I stood here, before you stood here, was there just masses of swampland? Did people find the camellia in the mud and pin it to their lapel? In Sedona, I once stood at the foot of cliff-faces and watched another white British woman tell me how ancient civilizations lived, how they built their homes out of the rock, how they grew crops and washed and washed and washed. She held a yellow legal pad in two fumbling hands and struggled to read her own handwriting as she recited the history. She did not know it like the back of her body, like the body of the land. I rescinded the old world. I renounced my name. I left the birthing hips never to return again. When my husband asks where to bury my body, where to bury our bodies together, where I will bury his body, he is planting me like a seed, so I swear the oath and hope to bloom. I ask to stay, to give my body to the ancient ground, I ask to stay, I ask to stay.

III

U.S Citizenship and Immigration Services: *Having a Green Card (officially known as a Permanent Resident Card) allows you to live and work permanently in the United States. The steps you must take to apply for a Green Card will vary depending on your individual situation.*

I am in love. I am an outlander.
He pulled me into his boat. We are in love.

before

Mother Tongue

My mother used to code-switch from English to Scottish,
from proper enunciation to an old lost tongue that she had put aside
at fifteen, and would shrug back on like a cardigan in the presence
of the women who tried their best to raise her. I did not like it
when she became Scottish, she seemed a fraud, painting her face
in the sapphire and ivory of the Saltire whenever rugby came on
the television. She seemed a sudden stranger to me, this person
from another country who recalled the wet streets of Drumchapel
after school and proudly set "Scotland the Brave" as her ringtone.

It is not lost on me that I too traded in my home country
for somewhere that they spoke my language just a little differently,
but I went in hope, not in fear to here. I take on their sounds like
good advice and hope never to sound English again. I aim to forget
fish and chip dinners where we watched Coronation Street
play on the television and took turns ignoring each other;
and eating Sunday roasts as my father kicked me hard under the table
for not eating quickly enough, or not eating the peas before the beef,
or not holding my knife every same second I held my fork.

Perhaps I can understand her trying back on the costume of her youth,
vying for her sisters' attention. I wish that she had noticed me there,
across the bar table in Govan, wanting so badly to go home again,
to be in the cottage we had shared, just her, my big brother, and me,
after my father began to rot, and left us to ruin. The first night
that we lived there, our life still in boxes, we all slept on one mattress

in her bedroom, It was just the three of us, before her old land could tear us asunder. Three people with a language known only to us, sharing a bedspread, lightning in ribbons outside, the television left on.

Wings

Grew up dysphoric—one eye on the sky waiting for planes that could bear me to new air, to a land with red-flag mailboxes & open-top Cadillacs that fit six; hands flared in the air.

At my windowsill, I surveyed the hedgerows & wilted. That place was all cider & cow shit & I was lonely, too loud for my family, shushed like waves. I didn't breathe: snared by air.

My birthplace was misplaced. I hung maps all over my walls & tattooed American cities on my arms, wistful embroidery. Stilled in Ilminster town square, summoned over the air.

At eleven, I wrote a class speech about the city so good they named it twice—I got an A+ & begged my mother for tickets. She murmured soon; I conjured skyscrapers in the air.

The first time a plane dropped me on the tarmac at JFK, I cried mouth open & unashamed. A fortnight would not quench my thirst—I drank in more than my share of the city's air.

I forget the prime minister's name, behind that coal door. I was not long for that land. I wonder if it's patriotism if you love another country: russet mountains and prairie air.

I was an ancient river, pulsing through my homeland, making a break for the Atlantic. I counted planes until I left—I'm going to be a part of it. Unanswered prayers lace the air.

Be Our Guest

A father asks for a public tribute
for a grandmother who has been dust for months
—her birthday: today. His typeset voice a whine,
he demands his daughter put her affection on display.
His ruddy cheek, his vast body, he wants grief that he can cash.
This wasn't her grandmother's way.
Nanny was her date for every family meal.
Nanny cut up her food for her until she was sixteen.
Nanny wrote cards and didn't know how to text
but open the door at number three, Orchard Vale
and the kettle was ever whistling.
That family is always celebrating death:
the day someone died, the funeral,
the birthday, the day the ashes were thrown into the stream.
Not friends, just family, so for this they're happy to convene.
Fractious in the car, they clink glasses in public houses.
They relish sitting, wielding the knife and the fork,
bearing down slicing until the bones are picked clean.

Tennyson Insurance

for Francesca

We were crooked bodies together,
feet out the windows of my Vauxhall Corsa.
Just husks after the winding day,
our aching hands holding cigarettes
to the soft burr of the lighter's flame,
dabbing off charred ends with aimless fingers,
forgetting the office behind us.

There, day after day, those relentless phone calls,
where I wore my headset like a helmet.
You played with the phone cord loops
like a teen girl on the stairs. There we were:
a team of two almost new together,
knew each other in an instant,
you eye-rolling the manager,
your blonde ponytail, our dirty mouths.

There, those hours were just hours between
when we put on our voices
to when we peeled them off.
There, we stepped outside to my car.
Nicotine and tar made breathing feel easy
and we could say that the money was worth it,
we'd make it if we could just scream out there.
There, where no one was listening.

When You Sit in the Pews of a Church, What Do You Pray For?

After Eve L. Ewing's retellings

I was channel-hopping curled in my mother's leather armchair, my teen body harnessed in blanket when my stepfather came home early from the pub alone some Sunday afternoon. Face erratic, he didn't see me until I asked from the bay window, "Where is my mother?" His skin blanched as if he had just realized that he went out in a pair & came home sliced apart. He murmured, "I left her, down the road, she was being impossible." I shoaled my feet in my mother's too-big slippers & slopped out the door - the soft felt whispering along the pavement as I went towards my expectations. She was wavering outside the newsagents, shouting incomprehensibly at traffic with wine glass eyes & *I closed my own with purpose & when I opened them she was silent & treading air so carefully, moving towards me with celeste eyes, & a soft mouth. She reached down & edged the slippers from my feet, tugging them onto her feet, washing one hand over my cheek. She floated up & the chardonnay from her body was back in its bottle. I can be a cork, my hands can plug it all.*

Code Brown

The year before I left England, I was supposed
to move. Moving is a lightness,
clear blue water that you can sink right into
and I love to just sink right in. Moving
is a BarcaLounger and I am Marty Crane.
Anyway, I was supposed to move that next day,
around noon, but it was four in the morning
and I was in a taxi cab. I was in Lancaster,
or I was when the taxi cab picked me up
outside the hospital in the ink dark,
with wet pajama bottoms and limp hair
like a slow misery. Then I was headed back
to my little stone cottage in Kendal,
where no one visited or even saw me unless
they passed by my incandescent window.

Except for that night because that night
I had to let in two paramedics
and watch as their caffeine-pale eyes
took in all the boxes, the air mattress
on the floor. I told them *I'm moving
in the morning* and I could hear them
thinking between them *are you sure
about that love?* All day long I had been
a tap dispensing, my stomach and throat
grunting and shifting like ancient pipes.
Something black had poured right out of me,
every twenty minutes from waking
until I stepped out of the ambulance
at the Royal Lancaster Infirmary.

I was looking around, trying to remember
the ambulance, for posterity, for a poem.
I don't remember it. I do remember
someone in scrubs at the hospital
putting me on a drip as I lolled
in a wheelchair in the corridor.

I remember being in a winged bed
clutching a cardboard sick tray
and a doctor saying *I'll just need
a quick stool sample*. As I went to get up
to go to the bathroom, he pushed two
gloved fingers into my rectum.

Perhaps that's what led
to the worst moment of that evening.
It wasn't watching the cute paramedic
wonder if I was being evicted or
retching in front of the cute paramedic,
or even the doctor telling me
you have a nice tear in your esophagus honey.
It was after they released me,
right before dawn, sitting in the lobby,
trying to figure out how to get home.
I coughed and felt my underwear,
my favorite-cotton-pastel-underwear,
filled up with shit like a sewer rising in a flood.

I waddled to the disabled bathroom,
washed with those green paper towels
that feel like emery boards, shed
my underwear into the sanitary towel bin,
wondering about leaving a note,
a paper apology for whoever had to collect it.
I'm sorry, I wanted to write, *I did shit myself,
but I promise I'm going to heal.*

Elizabeth, Everywhere

In me, there's a hole, near the size, and shape of you.
As if you and your body had come running right through.

I swore up and down—finger on the map—
once I stepped off that train I would never go back.

I erased your whole country with my love for you in it.
I can't remember how to be your daughter for even a minute.

Elizabeth, I don't care to try anymore, to brick up the spaces.
You drank the pubs dry. I built homes in distant places.

You are as much Glasgow as the buildings and bridges,
you still say *jayket* and *troosers*, you're lapsed but religious.

In you, there's a hole. It's the size of two figures:
me and my brother. Every year it's wrenched bigger.

Everyone can see it—that wound that gapes open.
Doesn't it hurt to breathe with a body that broken?

Where We Started
For Callum

I do not miss the stifled wet of English rain,
how I could never get dry or warm again.
I do not miss the stilted Sunday lunches
where family members took turns
in recalling each small embarrassment
of our childhoods. I do not miss eating
burgers and chips every day for three years
because our parents had owned a pub,
and we only ate what was cooked downstairs.

I do not miss all of the houses we had;
my small bedroom in Station Road
where the door did not close all the way,
or the cold floor in the cottage kitchen
when I was nine. I do not miss
the off-brand cola I would find
in the cupboards for Christmas,
a special treat picked up *just for me*.

I do miss dipping chips in hot chocolate
with my big brother in that stuffy room
upstairs at the Five Dials, cramming dregs
down the back of the armoire whenever
my grandmother was not looking, remains
found months later when mice appeared.

I do miss taking turns with my brother
to dip full length into an open barrel
of cold hose pipe water in the backyard,
squealing together. How my arms became
double-jointed because he twisted them
behind my back and I learned how to
wriggle free and gain the upper hand.

Or watching him skateboard up and down
on an immense broken door propped against

the back wall among a bounty of weeds,
waiting hopefully for him to break an ankle,
touching the inside of nettles carefully
with my forefinger so as not to get stung but still
ending the day in a bath laced with Dettol,
nettle welts circling my sunburned shins.

I do miss climbing onto the roof, just like
he showed me when the bar was bustling,
to read my paperback books in secret.
How we would case the fields sometimes
for yellow dandelions to feed our hamsters,
or his quiet fear of thunderstorms that I am sure
he would deny, or the way he would torture me
with claims of owl pie in airplane food
even as the throb of travel turned him green.

And how in the blue-dark as I read *Little Women*
or threaded headbands onto my tangled hair
to hide my uneven fringe, I never wished
for a sister. My brother and his unkindness
of elbows were enough company for the girl
in the book pile at the foot of the bedroom door.

The Hold-Steady

for Shirley Ann Bushby

I still save all the old recordings
my grandmother left on my voicemail
    I talked to her before I left—at her headstone
under the tree at the foot of the hill
and now that beacon is too far to walk
    I talk into the vacuum of air when I'm driving
or when I'm cooking or cleaning
silently when I'm arguing with my father
    my metronome—I hear her all the time
it's lavender where she is—no medication
no machine to empty out her blood
    to flush it and feed it back into her
I don't need to hear her quiet cursing
or hear her hum above ground
    when I'm reaching for her strength
—I hear it in the ways I come home
my name in her voice on the telephone

Little Town Blues
for Samantha

Cocooned in this body of sheet & linen   the paralysis made me powerless

but it was neat & warm there   There in my cast iron bed   there I could pretend

that New York was just outside   not the suffocating grey of the Cumbrian hills

After hours of bargaining   with myself   in that empty room

go to work   *just once* floor smothered by shampoo bottles & takeout boxes

I cried on the phone to my best friend   I hadn't seen her in months

I was homesick for her   not for home   I called her every day

she tethered me through the line   I pictured her   near my hometown

snug in her little brick house   only three hundred miles from me then

She told me I'm the biggest bitch she knows   laughter bubbles I was galvanized

first one foot   then another   until I was outside & breathing double time

at the wheel of my car   Yesterday's nightdress under last week's cable knit

playing Frank Sinatra   to muffle the whine of my clapped-out car   cry just twice

My office lanyard curdled my milk-white neck   My boots pinched my toes

but I made it there with brash tone & bluster   I could see they were made calm

by my slick of makeup   my perfectly rehearsed smile

Ode to Tony Soprano

You make me wanna fuck to please, gun to my temple
right on my couch, the way your sister did with that *stronzo*,
the jut of your lip, hard belly, throat bare and vulnerable,
throttled breath in your chest, snake eyes laughing *buchiach*.

Do I watch you in my underwear like this because you
remind me of my father, the blue moon in his eyes, how
he commanded a garage, men in overalls standing to attention
when he clapped a socket wrench on the top of his toolbox?

Or is it that your shit-eating grin is my ex-boyfriend's?
How his teeth ground as he viced my throat, spat in my face
as he rocked against me, waited until I was in the bathroom
before he'd snort a line off of his wrist, text some other girl.

Knowing them makes me get you, *you've got to burn to shine.*
You make me sick but you're all of them. When I wonder how
I loved those men I remember your wife wrapped in that mink,
the way your eyes fired the room and I kick off my underwear.

Calling All Cars

If I believed in someone up there, someone listening, maybe
I wouldn't have moved 262 miles from my friends who love me
so I could be 270 miles from the people who never knew how to.
Maybe when I drove to Hadrian's Wall I would have never
spit across the stone to let everyone know that   Glasgow can go to hell.
Maybe I'd remember that Glasgow *is* hell,
leaden rain, bodies in the street, bulletproofed shops,
and aunts who hold people by their necks.

If I believed in someone up there, maybe I would have taken
some time, after binge eating or masturbating on my couch
with the curtains open, to wring tears from my eyes like
a dishcloth, and admit I could not see the way forward,
that my body was struggling, flailing, falling apart. Yes,
if I believed in answered prayer, maybe I would have asked   somewhere in my unquiet,
for what I could never say out loud without jokes and asides.
Maybe I would have lain still in my bed, looking at the ceiling,
asking for help, believing that it would come.

Storage

While my gossamer dresses - still tagged - end up left in the doorways of charity shops,
I was packing my life into cardboard and paper and plastic bags from under the sink
and there's nothing. Nothing that I cared to keep except the things I think I should:
the bubble-wrapped bone china that once belonged to someone who mattered,
the painted furniture we once sprayed together with cans in the garden.
I think of the damp garage where my father will stack these boxes,
where one day I might be unpacking all the other crates
from sack-trucks. split-at-the-side suitcases,
of vinyl and running shorts and golf tees,
VHS tapes, their ribbons spooling out;
the things that make up my father,
the things that he kept.
And I believe that
held in my
hands

they will breathe.

To Greg, My Domino's Delivery Driver

Two years since I last met you at the heavy black door
of my building where you saw me in all my forms.
Dressed to the nines, other girls packed into my studio:
so small I had to balance a chopping board across the sink
to pour White Zinfandel into stemless glasses.
Slovenly and ruffled in week-old clothes,
with yesterday's takeout still on my breath.
Euphoric and smoking from my wide-open window,
ass cinched by the rungs of my victorian radiator,
then dashing down to meet you on the street.
Eyes red and mouth trying at a smile as I paid you
with palmfuls of pound coins, hair piled ragged
at my neck, apologizing for not giving a bigger tip.
Do you remember when you stopped by in the New Year?
No order from me in two weeks. You were worried. I was sure
I would die in that flat and you would be the one to find me.
Do you remember when I saw you on the garage forecourt?
You wrapped your arms around me like we were the oldest friends.
When I told my colleagues that, they looked at me like I had
two heads but sometimes when I didn't have work,
you were the only person I spoke to in a week.
You brought me chicken wings to three different addresses:
my ex-boyfriend's place with the winding staircase;
the townhouse where I holed up in the attic; and then that studio,
where I could reach the refrigerator from the bed.
Now I am the phantom of Oving Road.
You probably don't remember the last time,
when I told you I was leaving and you put
both hands on your hips in feigned exasperation.
I miss your laughing eyes, their creases, and their lines,
the way you knocked on my door, the sloop of your day-long shoulders.
Yes, I was the hungriest girl in England, and your pizza boxes
piled up waist-high under my electric meter.
When I let the power run out, I'd wait for you in the dark.

Before My Esophagus Tore and I Retched Black Blood

laundry overflowed the hamper, cigarette ash confettied my car seats
& my stomach was a gully full of chicken wings and macaroni.

Spent hours looking at plane tickets that I couldn't afford,
writing odes to Manhattan until my fingers began to flay pink.

I skipped work to stay in bed, always skipped drinks to sleep instead
& skipped sleep to eat at dawn & scream until my fists scrunched blue.

but then

I decided that the world revolves around me. Dirty hair
& unbrushed teeth: every sunflower bends to my light.
I shine all the time, especially when everyone is sleeping.

I write a hundred miles a minute. I decided to be the city.
I'll be the moons, the electric line on the horizon, the stars,
powdered air in alleyways, & fire escapes decked in ivy.

I wrote lists, made phone calls, I repacked my suitcase.
I decided that I will have America. I am all that I need
& now all my days & all my nights are spent living.

Leap of Faith

after David Hockney's paintings

WOLDGATE WOODS, 24-26TH OCTOBER 2006.
When I couldn't see the forest for the weeds, I would sink myself down into swathes of marigold and ochre, gold dust in the trees. I knew I would leave but somehow escape seemed bleak. The stumps of bark were pillars, and the skeletons of the canopies grew stronger and thicker as they pulled away from view, but the orange fur of leaf was rubbing under my feet, like trodden vines tying me to my roots.

GOING UP GARROWBY HILL, 2000.
Curious blue trees and skewed, strange heights: was it too far to walk or too high to climb? The patchwork of the fields was a blanket of breath, squeezed from me and I traced the looping lines of felt, would they lead me back to the start, to that first white scratch in the ground, or was this distortion a map, to my way out of these towns?

PEARBLOSSOM HWY, 11-18TH APRIL 1986 #2.
There'll be nothing but blue skies always on my mind, yes, I'll put this car in drive and leave the shit behind. The sky there is tiled over and the ground is graveled blur. The colors will kindle bright, glory glory in my straining hands, and as far as the eye could see: ferry boats, rain, sand. The West Coast was never in the plan, but England, England be damned.

onward

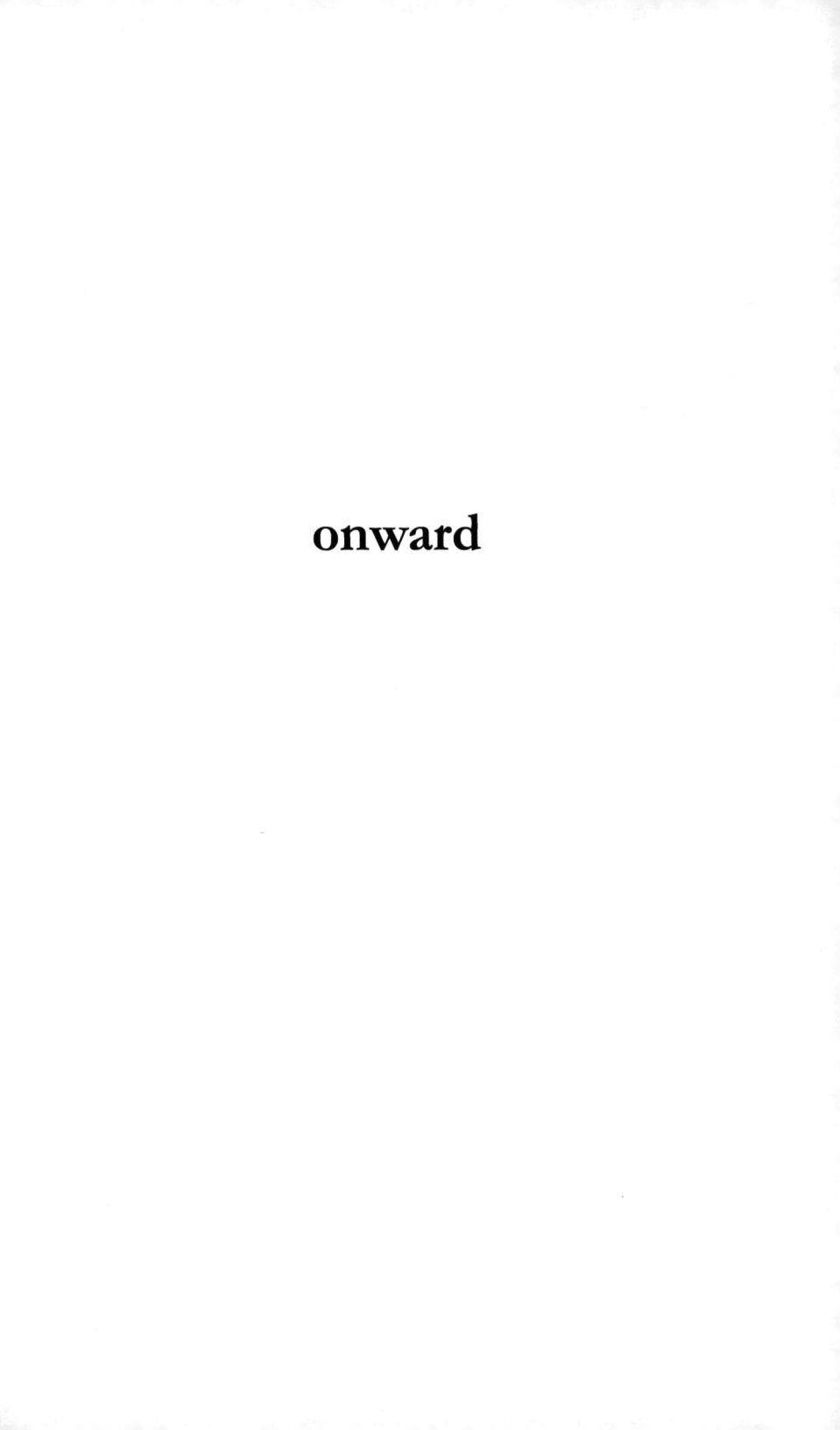

10th March 2020

    You didn't know life came in this form, full and blooming, a bower full of roses. The old life is faint in England. You think you will never return. Still, each day you walk a tightrope, thinking today will be the day some hand of the past will reach up and pull you back to those small towns with small people. You are twenty-seven and a newlywed. A year ago you didn't know this man or these places. You drink in the blessing, and how he makes every day new.

    A pandemic is coming along to knock everyone off their feet. Many are lost. You spend long days in a two-bedroom apartment. You put the phone down on your father. You put up a tent in the living room and watch time judder on. You miss your mother after six years of silence. You don't say so. People ask you how long you've lived in America because your accent is beginning to run and congeal, like butter in a glass dish left out in your 1970s kitchen. You watch the same television shows and repeat them two months later. You cry on your birthday but you are not homesick. You are sick of home. You don't want to hear its name again.

    Fun fact: It takes 2220 minutes to drive from Seattle, Washington to Lafayette, Louisiana without breaks. You can't drive to England. You could fly. Maybe you would never reach land.

Reading in the Tub
or "It's not where you come from, it's where you belong"

The states you've been to have a last name. I just read that in a Don DeLillo novel, that Oregon has a last name. I had to think about what that meant. I got my last name from my husband, and he got that from his father. Before I was a wife, my surname was inherited from my father and from my grandfather and way on back. Okay, the states have a last name. Is that the name given to them by some government official? Washington is the Evergreen State, so it would be Washington Evergreen? But Washington is named after a last name itself, right? I don't know, I'm from England. Do you think they care about presidents when they had a queen, nearly a hundred years old? She didn't have a surname. She did once. But not anymore. She didn't even have a passport. Perhaps the name comes from the person you know who lives there or lived there, the one that comes into your mind as you read this. My husband is from Buffalo, so when I think New York I think Wolf. It's pretty strange that I had New York tattooed on my wrist before we met, isn't it? When you hear Maine, do you think Stephen King? When I say Didion you say, California? When I say Sinatra you say—wrong! It's Jersey, remember? I know, I know. He didn't sing *Hoboken Hoboken*. Anyway, I read all that in this DeLillo novel: the one about the towers being cut through by aircrafts. And the figure falling through the sky. In the book it says something—I can't find the page—about living a life in a series of rooms. The office building, the apartment, the bookstore. I was in a gymnasium when I heard about it. He was in homeroom. What is so bad about a life in rooms? In these rooms, we share old stories and showers, and last names. The men in my family have never been to Louisiana, where we live now. Most of them have never been to Manhattan. If we ever moved there, we would list our last name beside the door of our building, and in a city of eight million, we'd just be two more faces.

Tabula Rasa

The Island demands a sacrifice   & here I am
You're beside me   snoring at eleven pm
Labor Day   You watched seven episodes with me
      bought me flowers just because
stayed couch-rooted   with a burning bad back
& watched Kate & Sawyer   fuck slow in a cage
before a rainstorm   because I like to watch
     people make cages of each other

     Let's get on a plane
It's not okay to say   I envy the plane crash
   I write down that the tension of the show
is that everyone is aching   Aching to escape
     but the audience doesn't want that
not really   When the raft that Michael builds
     is burnt down to the steel pontoons
the audience doesn't mind   We cheer

This baggage is so moveable   & immovable
     I had to leave the place where I was born
but I could never leave you   This cocoon we have built
an unexplodable hatch   Oh I could fill a book
     with the way this show makes my body feel
anything but lost   Found & seen & bound to you
There is no boat that could take us from the Island
     that will not always bring us back

Ode to My Husband's Toyota

You, his bonus best friend, his pen, his paper—you are his poem, your tan torqued frame, he crafts you like an artist. Indoors, I listen for the clink of his toolbox at the front door, the throttled roll of the spray cans as he comes in & out, covered in your corrosion, the skin he helped you shed, his forehead gleaming from the Louisiana heat, his eyes lit up. I'm still the forerunner of us two, the first thing he looks for in a room, & you are third to the party, our getaway car, our lifeline to the world outside of swamps and confederate flags, and tiny graveyards between stilted shacks. We marvel at how your windows peel away like a second skin, your roof opening to sky, your glass-back slipping down with one finger press

—together we are lifted up with the nightwinds.

After You Gave Birth

for Saxan

I suppose I needed to be looked after then, like the long hair
of a daughter which has never been cut. You hurried to my studio
when I called you sobbing, breathless when I thought I'd caught an STD.

In the same apartment, our stomachs wrenched from commitment,
we tried to laugh again. You always asked when I had last heaved my body
into the shower. I can hear you intone my name like a long-suffering mother.

—

When we met I thought you were a bitch. Turns out you had simply
been through hell. And also, you were usually being a bitch. Sometimes
we would crane our girl bodies over your desktop computer together

inspecting pink spreadsheets, wondering how we would ever survive.
Now that I am gone, I call you with no make-up on. Through the camera
I can see your freckles move when you laugh with your whole face.

—

You send me photographs of him on your chest and even under a veil
of sleep you are glittering. Your breasts hurt, of course. We commiserate
over blood and trees and all these years. Love, you have become

what we both were lacking. I want to know you and him together,
to see your patient hands swaddle and coax. I would take a plane
and a train just to see the mother that you have been all along.

New Year's Resolution
Bayou Shadows Apartments

Christmas lights are strung up
in our living room glowing
        but we aren't home right now
I made a promise to myself
        that I would climb mountains
with you this year   and so tonight
we're out climbing treadmills
You wear a cotton towel on your shoulder
 an epaulet   I tire early on
You catch my eye   in the mirror
sweat on the slope of your forehead
        I want to touch the cut of your jaw
Two polyester men jog between us
constant four feet clap   sharp grunting
one phone hands   free blaring spanish
the television runs silent neon
        Long before the hour's up
strip lights on a timer switch off
Nobody waves their arms   or stops
I train my eyes on blinking red digits
We keep on walking   you and me
and these strangers   a team
in this unrelenting dark
        this relief of blinkers
no need to see where we are going
We're going   then gone   walking
home together   Your voice a cloud
in my hollow ears   tiny bursts
from our late night brains: *That grunt*
Need water   *My ankle*   *Need a kiss*
        Don't want to work in the morning
So let's stay home My thumb
in the waistband of your shorts

I Don't Know What You Want Me To Say

I left and you can hardly blame me. I was just treading water, though
I did love that hill cased in silver shards where I slid to the bottom,
with my can of vodka red bull held triumphantly to the constellations.
And I loved the soft cobbles that pinioned my seventeen-year-old-girl stiletto
tapping and tutting, waiting for the cashpoint without our anoraks on. Here

on the Gulf, my fingers soak with ambition—I am becoming something else.
Though I say I miss the family I don't know how to lose anyone right.
They're all alive somewhere — grandmother in her bungalow steeping tea,
uncle in his back garden smoking hand-rolled cigarettes, grandfather
examining his model boats somewhere behind his heavy wooden door.

You don't ask me to stick around aloud—when I'm there you don't see me.
I'm no fit for the family picture you're painting and I am glad of that.
I remind myself every week it is kinder for me to leave and to stay gone,
make no waves, so there's room for you and the woman you claim to love,
her daughters squeeze-fitting the frame. I am cerulean and relieved in my absence.

When I was eleven you took me out to the River Isle at the town boundary.
They were building boxy identical houses that we still call the new estate now.
Beyond that still-there-fence, there was once only fields you said, and so
before I left I binoculared Herne Hill knowing it would always remain
—Yes, it was magic sometimes but have you ever looked across the Atlantic?

Kisatchie

Love me hard & fast on an air mattress
in the back of your truck in the woods
somewhere—as if we are teenagers—
near a dying campfire with melted
marshmallows in the crooks of my fingers
You have dirt smeared on your cheek
like some sexy bruised mechanic
or I don't fucking know Rambo
but anyway don't stop I love
that I'm wearing my oldest sweater
& I haven't washed my hair in days
& twenty minutes ago I took a piss
in a hole that you dug for me
but when you went down on me
just now the taste made you smile
& now your mouth is on my neck
& I can feel every breath churning
out of your chest into the pitch-dark air
with my name on your lips Every breath
is I love you so love me hard & fast
on an air mattress in the back of your truck
until we fall asleep & then love me lazy
& long on the air mattress in the back
of your truck when morning light splinters
& then fuck I don't know, love me deep
& slow back home on our living room floor over & over

                                                                                 again

Tale As Old As Time

In this one, the princess is not locked in a tower or a dungeon, not locked in at all, but is perhaps three hours away by car in a dorm room, or eight hours away by plane in a two-bedroom apartment with a man that the beast has met only once. Across the land, the beast still wields his grip, like a monarchy unyielding even as it dies out. The beast calls the princess and if she does not pick up, the beast brandishes his anger like a gauntlet around her bared throat. When the princess does pick up, she speaks too much, or too loudly, or about something the beast knows nothing about. And so, as if it was foretold the beast wounds her, snide and unrelenting until she is silent. Until she picks up but barely speaks. Until she stops answering at all and tells tales about other dragons she must fight, other kingdoms she must traverse. After years of curses and broken blood oaths, when she has shorn her hair and abandoned her silks and satins, the princess tells the beast that his reign is over: he cannot call anymore, he has been slain by her beating beating unquiet heart. The beast roars like her voice will destroy him: *the princess is disgusting, the princess will regret this, the princess will change her mind when she hears what the kingdom thinks of her.* She does not cry, she does not run, she does not lay her new armor down.

The townspeople warn:
girl, he is the only beast
that you'll ever have.

Eleven Delights from Lockdown

one I am learning to watercolor so we'll have something
to hang on the walls of a house we wish for years from now.
Maine seems so far away from this place of strip malls,
billboards & swampland, but when I reach out a hand
I'm pretty sure I can touch it: a New England peninsula,
shrimp rolls, cool, bare ankles on a Victorian veranda.

two I can smell the hydrangeas I bought you yesterday,
blue for democracy, *impeachment flowers,* we laughed:
some strange new word that we're sure won't stick.

three Your lips dust my skin before I've woken up each morning.

four I forget you're in the next room because *Lost* is on
& I'm somewhere beyond the sea. Then I remember
& spring up into your office, afternoon light filtering
through the toile, your head leaning back for my mouth.

five You mumble *I love you* when you're deep in sleep: a bedtime
ritual. I shrug off my bra & shrug on your low, sweet orison.

six I am trying to paint something with water & islands
& pine trees with these paints that you bought me.
I'm trying to flood my sheet with blush & muted dusk
like a flushed cheek. My brush sweeps an untethered land.

seven You kiss my neck as I pedal languidly on the fold-up bike.

eight You lay my pictures flat to dry on tissue. You say we'll frame
my art. I say *yes, & hang them high so they almost look good.*

nine You look like a painting in your Saturday cleaning clothes.

ten At least once a day one of us starts a sentence with:
in the Maine House, dismissing the concrete sky here.
Today it was you, after the delivery of your new truck tires.
In the Maine House, you said & my daubed fingers reached
for yours because it's real & tangible & yes, not quite there
but here under a roof of southern heat, you & I can see it.

eleven The hydrangeas are shedding already, but it's okay.
You collect the petals in your palm & float them
across the prairie of our kitchen in just one blow.

Memory of a Dragon

When I was nine, right about when
my parents were getting divorced
—my father cheated on my mother
with every woman he could coerce—

I went into school one morning
and came face to face with Mrs. S,
a parent. It was rumored she had
a glass eye. She was clearly pissed.

She was breathing so heavily it lifted
the hair off my forehead in short blasts.
She didn't like that I wasn't friends
with her darling daughter in my class.

And so she materialized in the cloakroom
before the day had even begun
to call me spoiled and selfish. My words
ran like a drain. My teacher had none

- yes Mrs. Mattravers, I do remember you
in the back lurking by the wall display
of the wizarding world, watching a grown
woman working me over the same way

a baker kneads bread dough. Usually, after
the last bell rang my mother would arrive
to pick me up in the car park. Today,
she stood waiting, with a smile like knives

because she'd heard, most likely from
my grandmother, whose garden stitched
the school's chain-link fence
and I'm sure I went and snitched

just as soon as I could. And so when Mrs. S
trotted up to the gate to look for her kid,
waiting for her was a Scottish woman
with large breasts and a handbag heavy like bricks.

*If you ever want to scream in my daughter's face
again, you'll need to come through me,*
said my mother in low tones, *and it'll be
the last thing you do, hen, I guarantee.*

It's the things you don't expect to miss that hit you hardest.

Taking Communion

Every night at the foot of our bed, your toes are silk;

the belly of a tulip. They hang over the mattress hillside

& my feet search out yours, seeking solace. Beloved you,

lacing your toes with mine in the coveted thrall of prayer.

In daylight, on our hand-me-down couch, I use my teeth

to coax the thick nail from each of your toes, daintily,

as if seated in some four-star eatery. You laugh all the time

& wonder aloud what people would say if they could see.

Every time I lift my eyes, your crescent moons

on the tip of my tongue, & ask *what people?*

After the Hurricane with Carly Rae Jepsen

                An email told us to come now   or not at all
                         to collect our things
          from the building where we teach English to teenagers
I had forgotten how to pilot the car   after so long in quarantine
  my ass   a couch cushion billboards   pulp along the highway
       Up three quiet flights   I expected to find no ceiling
          but the lights came on when I asked for them
                I packed up books and notes
    into a wheeled suitcase   a paper bag   a plastic crate
              It took two climbs to get it all
           The trees were snapped in half like necks
      in the faculty parking lot friendly faces floating around
      Today talking aloud was like breath inflating a chest
warm and sweet like pastries   or an arm around a stomach at dawn
              so we talked until time ran out

                Now I am back on the highway
   paying close attention to everything   so I do not see it coming
     As my Hyundai summits the overpass   there is a flood
      coming at me   carried not on water   but on wind
        A car swerves as I strain my eyes to see it
                   It is a wave
                  of pink balls
              styrofoam or sponge
              I drive through them
              The radio jerks on
         and I want to cut through the clouds
  I feel the sudden urge   to break through the ceiling
    I feel the apples of my cheeks   I feel rosy
   light opens up on the plain   a splash of castor oil

The Vulnerability of Estrangement

It is like having the lights out in all the rooms except the one in which you sit. Yes, you are sure that people still go on living out there, in the darkened spaces, but there is only you under lamp spark: working through the night, becoming something new. It is strange to imagine answering the telephone, hearing aloud there's no longer anybody home. Do you think you'd recognize his headstone, or that you'd walk right by? She could move, you'd never know where she went.

Sometimes it seems as though you'll never see Ilminster again.

It is strange to be gone, blown away like the roof tiles in a Louisiana hurricane. You could sit on your stoop, smoke a Marlboro down to the letters, try to recall how he smelled in the coffee shop, pointing out the windows, stealing palmfuls of your chocolate muffins. Or how her hands felt, as you lay in her lap, searching your hair with a metal comb and careful fingers, for tiny living animals you had brought home from school. There's just no use in recalling how it all came apart.

If you turned out those lights, you cannot languish in the dark.

Unconditional
for Lilly

I haven't been writing much lately. My body keeps the score, as they say, of all the ways and days I'm failing. I have it all, you see and so I spend my time, like money: in abundance. Watching time ebb away, watching the leaves on the trees change from ever-ever-green to hot-to-the-touch red. And I try to muster up the feeling in my legs to walk a straight line from my car door to the classroom or to the grocery line. Wrists quaking under the weight of my unfinished lists. I see myself from outside my skin: canceling dinner plans, watching my legs splay on the sofa, ignoring my phone because I don't have a smile left in a pocket somewhere to pull out and put on. It is strange that every day can be a happiness, yet there is still a seed in my brain, begging for water, ready to burst. I hate nature poems. I like poems that feel like a person, that feel like a fight. I like to picture two lungs squeezing and releasing like the day was too damn hard. Of course, it is easy to write this, now, when I am escaping the mist, when I am pulling free, knowing quietly I will return. It is just easier to be crazy, now I know that love will never leave.

4th April 2021

Just when you think you know it all, time reminds you it is not done with you yet. Not even close. People leave, and people come back. Some people you send away and take in that great relief like a drowning woman takes in her first uncluttered breath. America is not a miracle cure but it is peonies wrapped in brown paper, chocolate from fresh pastry on your mouth, the sun on your back in a beer garden. You put the phone down on your father for the last time. You move to Denver, a place you've only driven through before. The distance pulls at you childishly, wanting its way, wanting your head bowed and your feet returning in your own old footsteps as if you never left. You're laughing now, writing that, because in what world would you go back? Look at the man beside you. Know he was there all along. It's silly you took so long to get here.

Fun fact: He was born in a hospital in Niagara Falls. He was born 932 days before you. You were born 3456 miles from him. You came late, your mother complained. You were born on your paternal grandfather's birthday instead of your maternal grandfather's birthday. What does all of that mean? Why am I asking you? You were always awful at math.

In the seventeenth episode of *Lost*, titled "In Translation," John Locke says: "Everyone gets a new life on this island, Shannon. Maybe it's time you start yours."

When I Cut Ties With My Father, My Family Forgets Me Like I'm Fiction

So—let me remind you:

When I was fourteen, I went out for a meal with my father.
I couldn't finish my dinner. When we got back to his place
—above a gas station—he grabbed my hair by its root,
pulled me to my knees and made of them a sled, dragging me
from the white lines of the parking lot, up the steep stairs
to the rough carpet of the room he had painted sky blue for me.
I locked myself in while he battered the door with small fists.
I opened the window and tested my weight on the canopy
above the gas pumps. I weighed up sprinting to my grandmother's,
a block away. Perhaps I was scared he would hurt her too,
or that she wouldn't open the door in time or open it at all
if she knew he would want her to keep it closed.
So, I learned how to talk my way out of anything
and over a decade later, I found scissors big enough to cut ties.
Now the very same people who watched him beat a child black and blue
tell me he's just a man who loved his mother and did the best he could do;

and shame on me for not respecting my father.

What is This Place, If Not a Nest?

for Amy

When we were twenty-two, we lived like sisters,
Amy and me. One of our evenings limb-heavy
on the sofa, we found something at the front door
of our townhouse. Small and black like a doorknob,
we heard its shrillness from deep inside, long before
we opened up to search the gloom. It was a blackbird.
Small as a balled-up fist. No bigger than a Christmas
tree bauble. She was alone, but defiant, using her voice.

I've lived my whole life in cardboard boxes. I always
preferred it that way. At Strawberry Field, I took
the smallest room and skipped work on weekdays
to cry on the couch. I helped Amy move in, packing
her whole life into the boot of her car, wielding
a bookcase like a weapon. The hill to our house
was a colossus and we held our collective breath
as the car squealed up to our duck-egg door.

I stacked boxes and bags at that front door, muscles
in my back machining from memory. The doorstep,
that was where we found the bird. We called her Bella.
Amy was scared to touch her. I was scared to take her
away, thinking her mother might be waiting for her
somewhere in a hedgerow to fly back home. We dialed
numbers until we were invited to sanctuary an hour away.
We scooped her into a box, left on a pilgrimage.

Our house was a sanctuary for a while. It wasn't
a year before it was time to move again. So I left
Amy and the town where I grew up, to share
an apartment with a stranger in Portsmouth
who told me that he'd been in prison but
wouldn't tell me why. One night he lost his keys,
buzzed the door in the cruel dark. He pushed
into my bedroom, used my body like a handle.

I left my wooden bed behind when I made my getaway.
In the car Bella rode like a queenly ball of feathers,
throned on Amy's knee. Bella talked the whole way
there. Amy, nervous like a bird too, held the box
with marmalade fingertips. We drove into the swollen
night and at the end of it, Bella was safe in some
cotton wooled nest and we were back at the townhouse.
Today, I'm five thousand miles from Amy.

When I move now, nothing gets left behind, and even if
it does, I can always buy it again but I cannot buy the way
my husband's chin dips onto his chest in languorous sleep
as our cats rough their faces into his open palms. Amy
is moving soon. I wonder if her new home will have
our same Friday night wine glow without our old battered
couch and the hula hoop wrapped in twinkle lights. I wish I
could help her pack though we both know I won't come back.

She remembers Bella:
the way we touched her feathers like she was leading us home.

Are All The Fathers In Your Poems Real?
after Aimee Nezhukumatathil

If by real you mean as real as the stinging light still burning
in an empty refrigerator, the pooling on a water-ringed table,
the crumple of a toe against a desk's steel leg—
then Yes, every last page is true, every sharp word,
bark and bitch. Wait, I have made them all up—all of them—
and when I say I am fatherless, I mean my father was less
and so somewhere there is a room full of fathers, all of them.
Can you imagine the number of beater cars, how many
unearthed golf balls? Even now, my fathers prepare to call me.
One dials the phone, another commandeers the speaker.
One screams into the abyss of the internet and one sits
at my grandmother's grave. One sleeps with his broken glasses
on, another is preparing a dinner alone and every single
one of them wonders why I am never coming home.

Nothing But Memory is Left
Rocky Springs Ghost Town, MS

Is it a sin to compare the quietude of the country church
to the solace of this campground restroom? Palatial with high
ceilings painted the color of caramel whip, glossy tiles scrubbed
clean by some absent hand. Even the window beams in light
or the light streams out, perhaps it is corrugated plastic but
the light gleams yellow just the same as a stained glass window
& then, of course, there is the electric light high up on the wall,
a bar of slow rhythmic pulse, a throb just the same as some
hymning hum. From my seat on the toilet, it has that same
chapel smell, musty like a bookshop, & what is reverence
if it is not rows & rows of bookshelves in a warmly bathed room?

I think back to the chapel, an hour ago, a small brick church
in a ghost town that once had a population of more than two
thousand. There is nothing of the town now but trees
& a rusted safe, preserved & labeled, but a sign says there are
services at the church twice monthly. We let ourselves in & stood
at the pulpit, read from the open page about Moses
so that our collective voice shook the sanctuary.
When Thornton went outside to relieve himself, I sat in a pew,
second from the front, & clasped my hands as I used to do
on my lunchbox on a folding table in Greenfylde Primary School,
three thousand miles from here. In my prayer, I gave thanks
& asked for nothing at all, because everything that I want
is already in reach, & my arms are long & grateful. Perhaps
I do not believe in god but I do believe in something.

Before we left the church to come to this campground,
where I sit now, we walked the graveyard & read off the names.
Lillie Winters & her family. A number of Lums scattered around.
These people from the 1800s would be forgotten if there were not
a place to keep their names. *We must be buried, not cremated,*
I tell him all the time. One eight-foot obelisk bears a short poem.
I read it aloud to Thornton, our smallest fingers linked in solemnity:
Thus the human heart's bereft, & nothing but memory is left.
I repeat it now, as I wash my hands. It cannot be a sin to compare
the church to this room. Am I not heard here just the same?

When people ask: *How would it feel to move back to England?*

I want to say, in a tight unfamiliar voice, have you
ever felt like you lived in a landlocked state
and you couldn't forget how the air feels on the coast
the breathless rush of wind, the salt on the backs
of your hands, the sand on your wrists and your ankles—
I dream it so vividly sometimes, me
trapped again in a room in my father's bungalow.
It's always there: my desperation to return to the rush
and the swell and the tangles of seaweed as vivid
as my black hair in wrought ribbons. At ten
I stumbled from the water, blood pouring
from one leg as I blazed gold on two cheeks, believing
I had been dashed on the rocks like a shipwreck
from one of those old paperbacks I carried everywhere.
In the dream, I sit on the bedroom floor
try to recall the water enveloping my feet, making a pair—
of the shore and me. In the dream, I sit on the floor
and bang my head against a bookcase like that would
pull me back across the sea. It would feel like
suffocating, it would feel like a death in the family.
But I don't say all that. I just shake my head politely,
gesture at America with two open hands and say
I'm sure it would be fine but I'm not going anywhere.

I Can Forgive You

for my mother

After my father tossed me around his flat
like a rag doll, and I came home and threw
the house phone down a flight of stairs, you sat
at the dining table and waited for me to finish.
Sometimes we danced around that dining table
not boogying but bad ballroom dancing,
heads thrown back: *It's all about your frame!*
Crashing into chairs, singing to Stevie Wonder.
Or Lionel Richie. Or George Michael. Or Celine.
At night I would sit on the closed toilet seat
and talk to you while you bathed in our tub.
I had a child's cruelty when I would talk about
your brick-heavy breasts. You would say,
wait until you're my age, yours will be just like mine.
Our bathroom was always ice cold.
At least once a week I snuck into your closet
for your wrap-around sweaters or chunky boots.
I can still smell that leather, eight or nine shelves
Filled and double stacked. I think the last pictures
I have of us together are from that day in the snow,
me clutching two chocolate bars from the local shop,
you in a winter jacket, sticking out your tongue,
cropped hair ruffled, grinning like you knew me.

—

I carry my weight in the same places as you,
stomach and hips cracked thick with age,
and my breasts, they need wire, just like you warned.
I can't forget the ways that you hurt me
but I can forgive you enough to remember all this.

We are all writing about the moon actually

Even when we are supposedly writing about crushes and being crushed;
indolent fathers and indulgent mothers; there is always a push and pull.

Sometimes it is violent like the red rope of love that holds a baby
to the womb. Sometimes somber and slow like the tug of a handkerchief

from a pocket at a wake. But there is always this ebb and flow. My stomach
faces the door. My shoulders twist to you. My ass hurts like a motherfucker.

I fell on the ice today. Every night around this time, there is a shaft of light
that falls on your face. I wait for it. An expectant sky waiting for the moon.

It comes tonight and your breath lifts the cover. In your dreams
I am taller than you and I wrap tinsel around your wrists and elbows.

In your sleep, you murmur something that sounds like a love letter
But is probably a recipe for slow-cooked corned beef. This pull from you,

this push to me, it reminds me of the moon's aching symphony. No,
it doesn't remind me. It's just there in everything we are writing.

How can I leave you now? When you are always drawing me back.
I turn to you in the dark. Your petal neck tells me you are here. Yes,

that is what I always do. I turn to you in the dark, my feet in your shores,
my weak hands reaching out to the depths of your sweet brass heart.

On My 29th Birthday

Four cards in the mail at our new house in Denver.
One after six years of ballooning silence.
I recognize her handwriting with such ease.
My new name and new address
swooping and looping in black biro.
I save her card until last.
One from my best friend, a crude joke.
Abstract dandelions from my aunt, sand and violet.
Another: "granddaughter" in red like a profanity.
I take my mother's card in two hands,
eyelashes shaking, new brick house shrinking.
Pink cheeks betray me to an empty room.
Once I would have sent back to her
an envelope embroidered with nettles,
cyanide, clenched fists.
But here, in our century-old house,
hardwood floors we dance on in
bare feet, met by candlelight and books:
I swallow the old rancor.
Her card is upbeat and breezy.
Meaningless words. Good intentions.
Between the lines in ink just for me:
In me, there's a hole,
near the size, and shape of you.
As if you and your body
had come running right through.
I take up my pen.

Ode to My Husband's Ass

Sweet swooning slopes like long drives on Sundays: makes me want to tie up my hair in a silk scarf and put the roof down, apply lotion to the soft skin around my eyes and take a sip from a warm, flat soda, abandoned in the car cup holder for a weekend of hammocks and wrists laying lazy in the shallow bed of the river. When I was eleven or twelve we would paddle shin deep in the stream that bisected Waterlake Road. The others would grow tired, climb back up to the footpath, and I would remain, trespassing into the dark hollow where the tepid light could not pervade the thicket of trees and I could see myself in the water; big green eyes and cracked elbows. Now, you look back at me, your fingers dipped in the pages of a book, your mind somewhere else. My hand smoothes a path from the small of your back to the gully of your thighs. *It feels like summer*, I say. *I want to swim.*

To All The Towns I Loved Before

It's not you, it's me. On Twitter, Maureen Langloss posts a photo:
two flowers growing in a wall *I hope someone puts them in a poem.*
I would do it but I am sanding a stepstool in the backyard right now,
sawdust on my thighs and my cheeks. It was cheap, from Ikea when I
still lived alone in England. It came over in a shipment with all the things
I'd forgotten I owned, the covered footstool I bought in Chichester
when I first tried playing house, all the books from all the car boots
and library sales and paperbacks that foolish friends had lent me.
My grandfather's lamp, musty shade and all. Vases, all empty.

There is something about those flowers in the photograph though:
how the wall is ruddered with cracks that might bring the whole thing down
But the flowers are bolstering, supporting, cradling. They are load-bearing.
Must not be taken down. I call to mind a stone building from my hometown,
once a grammar school for girls in Ilminster. Built in the 1500s, overlooking
St. Mary's Church where I once faithfully trooped in with my classmates
to sketch the stained glass windows, the memorials carved in stone.
The stone of the school came from Ham Hill. I wonder if flowers
usurp the walls and windows, interrupt the people who live there now.

It hasn't been a school for years and I haven't been the same in a long time.
There is still snow on the ground here and the backs of my wrists are cold.
I do not put my coat on yet. I want to feel the benefit. My grandmother
always used to say that. My other grandmother once visited me
in a cottage in Kendal where I had considered killing myself daily. I
don't recognize that girl or that house, open wounds and mottled pores.
Now I can be a purple pink bloom flushed with sun, ambushing
passersby at dawn, shaking sediment from walls, blooming wild,
reaching out, shaking rock, asking: which of you still recognizes me?

Homecoming

      Our month of honey has stretched into years, never waning.
We lay in bed watching the afternoon's rain cleave the sky.
      Oh, when will our lilac hearts be this full and fearless again?
Later in the garden as I wait, underdressed, for our dog to shit,
      I see the delicate jaws of a sunflower groan open like an ache.
The yellow: our bright future. The burst: our copper bodies.
      We once fell to our knees under moonlight. We still have that,
amongst brick walls and subway tile and the smell of garlic.
      I call England home aloud but you know when I tug your collar
at a bar that it is really where we lay our heads together
      The corner covered with ivy where you brew coffee, humming.
The breakfast bar where I read to you from a heavy cookbook.
      Later, we read on the floor of my study, intermittently interrupted
(I learn French from my phone by dwindling lamp light,
      and you Wikipedia fifty-year-old environmental disasters.)
When you rise to your knees, you kiss my pearl-white hand
      as if you're proposing all over again in this paperback fort.
I wish we could watch this picture show from outside:
      see ourselves in my study, bathed in amber light, surrounded
by this nostalgia for something that we plan to keep.

Roots

I will never know when the pain was over.
It was not a storm that blew up the sky
with a sharp constellation of embers
that died down like tenderness while I slept.

It was not a ten-car pile-up on the highway:
each wreck collected and hauled away,
ghosts made of the traffic, until even
the marks on the road were rubbed into dusk.

Nor was it a bright day where the greedy sun
pushed at our pale backs with an eager keening
that would streak sharply away, replaced quietly
with afternoon hangovers and the glitter of early slumber.

It was never all fixed. It was never made easy.
Every day still can present a cobbled street.
I simply take off my heels, go barefoot to my blessings.
The tallest linden tree in Denver is in *my* backyard.

I count wins from our couch, exercise in the dark,
scratch my bug bites on the Iceberg Pass, drive
right off the road. I am never quiet here but if I was,
no one would ask me how my voice was quelled.

You know, a country does not a mess, undo.
A country cannot make bad things untrue.
I grow ivy and strings of pearls, and my hair too,
until my bony elbows are dressed in waves.

When planes fly above me now, I spread my arms,
pad across my own lawn, curl my toes with each step.
I am lighter somehow. The load I shrugged off,
left somewhere, luggage in a forgotten hold.

I am not *going* home. I have made it *here*, anew.
Piles of golden leaves, creaking floors, wool slippers,
his feet on my lap, my books on every surface,
sweet petrichor winding through the screen door.

I take a fallen branch, spread it across our wooden table,
measure the veins in the leaves against the purples
and blues under my skin. I strike a match, touch it
to a candle, to a linden flower. Its kindle cracks a rhythm,

a train that has found its tracks:
I belong. I belong. I belong.

Acknowledgements

A number of these poems (or previous versions of them) owe their start to these incredible literary magazines: *Stanchion, Anti-Heroin Chic, Bending Genres, Daily Drunk, Discretionary Love, FEED, Gravel, Great Weather for MEDIA, HAD, JMWW, Kissing Dynamite, Moist Poetry Journal, MoonCola Zine, No Contact, Olney Magazine, Poetry Super Highway, Sledgehammer Lit, Stillpoint Literary Magazine, Roadrunner Review, Twin Pies Literary, Willawaw Journal.*

Thank you to Ariana D. Den Bleyker for believing in this manuscript and championing it, and for your friendship! My deepest gratitude to Luna Vallejo-Howard, Rachel Pittman, and Sarah Harshbarger for your care in reading and workshopping this manuscript, and to the writers who took the time and effort to blurb this collection: Dan Brady, David Kirby, Eric Nguyen, Gauraa Shekhar, and Tara Stillions Whitehead; I am so grateful for your meticulous and tender support of my work.

Thank you to my former professors and friends: Lisa Vandenbossche, David Swann, Michael Horner, Amy Fleury, and Keagan "Keags" LeJeune, as well as special thanks to two early teachers: Andrea Jones, who began my love of reading, and Madeleine Birch, who advocated for my education, and was on my side when even I wasn't. A note to my many students, past and present: I continue to be so proud of you all and excited to see all the good you're going to do in the world.

Gone too soon are Katie Yeomans (née Hall) (1991-2023) and Gauraa Shekhar (1995-2022) who are never far from my thoughts. I am grateful to have known and loved them both.

To old and new friends, and longtime supporters: Nicholas Higginson, Natalie Wilson, Monica Fuglei and family, James Malzard, Charlotte Bevan, Jessica Williams, Mordecai Martin, Dave Gonzales, Karen Hobbs, Maegan Gonzales, George Egan-Ballard, Katie Stevens, Alejandro and the rest of the Suntay family, Libby Patrick, Elliot Alpern, Nathaniel Berry, Robert Vaughan, Meg Tuite, and of course, Erin Elizabeth Smith and the *Sundress Publications* team. I am thankful for you all.

With love and thanks to my first American family who brought me to the US and gave me my first home here, Carli, Case, Lilly, Michael, Daisy, and Drew.

To my family, some of whom are no longer with us: my grandparents: Shirley Bushby, Gill Austen, and Jim Bushby; my mother Elizabeth Tucker who fed my hunger for books ceaselessly and my stepfather, John; my auntie Jane, my uncles Jed, Simon, Paul and Danny; Michelle Power, my "Auntie Chelle," for her unconditional love, and for the gift of my very favorite cousins, Sam and Jake; and finally, Aunt Melody and Uncle Jim - marriage has truly blessed me with you both as family!

Thank you to my darling brother Callum Packer and his wonderful other half Faye Dodd. And thank you to my beloved friends: Francesca Main, Tara Stillions Whitehead, Sarah Harshbarger, Amy Goss, Saxan Monro, and Samantha Warren, and all of their partners and babies and animals. You are the family that I chose and however far away I go, I'd choose you all again.

I thank my girls Pickle, Nora and Claudia Wolf, for always being by my side.

Most importantly, I thank Thornton Wolf, my husband, my American Dream. I love you. The way that you love me has changed my whole world.

About the Author

Shannon Wolf is a British-American writer and teacher, living in Denver, Colorado. She received a joint MA-MFA in Poetry at McNeese State University and also has degrees from Lancaster University and the University of Chichester in the UK. Her poetry, short fiction, and non-fiction have appeared or are forthcoming in *Bending Genres*, *Heavy Feather Review*, and *The Forge*, among others. *Green Card Girl* is her debut poetry collection. You can find her on social media @helloshanwolf.